Entering the House of Awe

Susanna Childress

New Issues Poetry & Prose

A Green Rose Book

New Issues Poetry & Prose
The College of Arts and Sciences
Western Michigan University
Kalamazoo, Michigan 49008

First Edition, 2011.

ISBN: 978-1-936970-00-1 (paperbound)

Library of Congress Cataloging-in-Publication Data:
Childress, Susanna
Entering the House of Awe/Susanna Childress
Library of Congress Control Number: 2011924069

Art Direction: Tricia Hennessy
Design: Sam Adams
Production: Paul Sizer
                   The Design Center, Frostic School of Art
                   College of Fine Arts
                   Western Michigan University
Printing: McNaughton & Gunn, Inc.

Entering the House of Awe

Susanna Childress

New Issues

WESTERN MICHIGAN UNIVERSITY

Entering the House of Awe

Also by Susanna Childress

Jagged with Love

Amado mio—

Contents

I.

Marvelous Truth
confront us
at every turn, in every
guise, dark horse,
egg, iron ball, shadow,
cloud of breath
on the air.

—Denise Levertov, "Matins"

What's Done

Lord   about the women who pummel their children
in public   Sweet Jesus
both you and I been angry enough to shake a baby to turn over tables   Lady

at the airport flinging her spatula of a girl again   and again
into a chair   SIT loud enough to render an ocean still only
she isn't   she wails You saw

the one in the grocery store dangle her son by an ankle   drop him
head-first into her cart Like Peter he stayed upside down
squalling and I swear   I was a pillar of salt in the aisle

          The problem   Almighty

is what Janet's mother said of French-kissing teens   *Do* that *for the world to see
and you've got to wonder what's done in private*   This is not loaves and fishes
is not the white stone on which you'll carve our new names   this is

the lopped-off ear   the hem of your gown after all those years
of blood   You   send us hell-bent upon each other   each
lurking bully quite sure of representing Capital-Y   So I can ask

          you

(as my mother would say   swatting   the air to keep her fists from me   O *you*)
with your feathers   who bends but a portion of our hearts
toward hell   Let the lettering of their oversized T-shirts

spell out our own failings Holy One   about the women
who have no shame   Split open the hazelnut under
our ribs   Let there be enough to go around   and around

The Green Spider

I will take your mind off the things you think of only
in the shower—space cleared by an egg-shaped soap turning over
in your hand, by the white tile, the wet sheets down

your length. You might have thought of the seven children
in Madagascar whose parents were taken with no
explanation, the children walking each day

past the prison until one of them lobbed
a stolen fish through the bars for his mother, for which
he was shot: once in the hip and once in the ear. Or

perhaps the woman in Utah who buckled her daughter in
for a ride to find the girl's father, her cheating husband,
catching up with him outside a paint store and running

him over, and backing up, and running him over,
and backing up and running him over until, according
to witnesses, he stopped screaming and lay, spilled

as the canisters of Alaska Bay Blue purchased for his new
home. I will even take your mind off the teller in your mother's bank
who swiped $3 from accounts late on various afternoons

for over a year and would've made a clean break but for
the octogenarian who hit the bank president over the head
with her purse for nine weeks of miscalculations

and the $27 she could not do without. Today
the chamber of your shower is hallowed with the smell
of lathered hair, equal parts ginger and goat's milk,

and though I find no joy in deceiving you, I will: so small,
translucent and green you'll forget these things, the slow crimp
they might have made in your understanding

of peril and need so that instead you'll bend
close and stare, think how intricate
the world is, how delicate and composed.

The Wry World Shakes Its Head

A Meditation on Isaiah 40

The first time you see *the rugged place become a plain*
is the moppy red hair of your mother's retarded cousin

Roy Dale, cropped, stern as a recruit, something of a joke
atop his docile body: slack, spittled, set in the corner

with cross-legged abandon by Shirley Ann, his sister,
for whom you hope *every mountain and hill shall be*

made low since she's baring more than details of last week's
breast enhancement: blood, stitches, pus and pain—that bitch,

which she fought through to give Roy his cut since
the last bastard with clippers must've been blind, or at least, she says,

fucked-in-the-head as Roy! Mother gasps, Shirley Ann laughs,
almost shouting, and without warning you, too, are laughing,

oh you're laughing, something of that same joke,
the woman's sense of irony, *the glory of the Lord revealed*,

and Mother gives you a deep blue commandment
in the scint of her eye: Sober Thyself. A corner of you

knows to fold, for sweet Lucille, her pickled life, you sober,
dear Aunt Luce who cried out, *Speak tenderly to me!*

but she didn't cry out, died in a wild-eyed stupor, unable
to prove it was Shirley Ann who tapped cocaine into her hospital

cup. Roy Dale broods through a bag of shelled pistachios
and turns again, *Look, Faye. Faye. Got my hair cut, Faye,*

lookit, and my mother, without fail, deems him handsome before
Shirley Ann yanks her back to *They been saying* and *Look here, she*

changed her own damn will and so forth. You have stopped
being here, with Mother, the acidic flicker inside you says

lookit: Bentley died young, left Lucille with a girl (not yet
turquoise brassiered) and a bovine toddler the doctors called

not so bright. Why the whole lot didn't *proclaim her hard service*
completed, her sins paid for is more than you can ask,

but here you all are anyway, funeral four weeks past,
Shirley Ann's God-awful chunk of money, the shorn red

head of Roy Dale, your mother, reluctant emissary
of the family, *making straight in the wilderness a highway.*

And you, let's not forget, your mother's own dark daughter,
a buffer, opening another bag of nuts for Roy while Shirley blows

her top, Shirley, tattooed, orange with tan, Shirley, said
to have blamed herself, to have bawled herself ill when her

three-year-old brother, unattended, drank Drain-O and scoured clean
his grey-soft brain. The wry world shakes its head

but what is it they want? Comfort, comfort, only you are not
His people and if by chance you are, you're shot through

with withering, field of flowers, plain of grass, the Lord's hand
giving doubly, doubly for sins and now Mother has begun to cry,

Roy Dale announces, again, his haircut, and Shirley Ann's breasts
splotch red as holy text. Where, then, to go from here? Back,

you think, the shadow must go back ten steps
on the stairs, not before birth but just after, that first

brusque shout, not *What should I cry out* but *What shouldn't I?*

Mother as Water-Damaged Book

Late in October the rains came, angry as a muzzled dog,
        destroying seven boxes of my books. Mother
tells me at Thanksgiving after I've found the gray floret

of mold, a puckered Thoreau, Neruda, Joyce
        Carol Oates belly up on the washer, *I was*
drying them out for you, she says, and a great feral

weight slips from her eyes, rolls
        helplessly like cobble into a stream,
to her knuckles bending and scurrying over hundreds

of marred pages. Without warning, the entire
        basement covers itself in open books, Sappho
propped on a broken blender, Sor Juana in facing

translation, my golden-edged Pocket Sonnets
        tentative as upturned palms on the VCR, four
fat Nortons halved to breathe atop 2x4s at the window. When I start

to cry—my fingers uncertain how to touch
        the *Moby Dick*, the *Complete Emily* I'd marked up
in school, Dr. Marj Elder having lent 48 years to the ink

in my margins now kaleidoscopically sprawled
        like the place in hell they put Hermann
Rorschach—my mother also begins to cry. The splendid loops

of Gwendolyn Brooks' signature, penned on my birthday
        the year she died, now a pirate's
eyebrow. Upstairs the timer sounds once more, reminding

my mother of the afternoon I came home electrified
        with news: how the heart is always
beeping, sixty a minute, *even fast asleep*, my small fist

surging, Beep-beep, Beep-beep, like that. Above us, the turkey,
        the potatoes and stuffing, the paella
in its pan thick as a chapter, brown in the oven's dark box.

The Lanterns

They have played me the tapes, ones sent after Gran died,
bubble-wrapped in a box with pictures of my mother

and father, newly wed. I left the songs we sang, left my sister
behind and began by myself into a hazy land of words,

all its red doors open to the two-year-old. In my mouth, the tongue
was a wand of sounds. Hearing them now, how I worked

through the brambles of language in a perfectly joyful swipe,
it's as though I prayed without knowing I prayed, started all over

with the sweet ache of not remembering myself but knowing
it is me long after the demulcent edge, my innocence spent

in heaven, as Wordsworth would have it, before I was born. The gods
of the world wrapped themselves in my mother's credulous

laugh, her limbs giving as stalks of wheat, her lap the whole
moon, and my father's voice, stentorian, big-beared, searching out

our shrieks of enchantment; his body, too, a castle. I was also lovely,
his pequeñina. It is not foolish of me: surely I was lovely. I hear

the awe of my voice at itself, spilling from the tender napkin of my throat,
ticks and shirks of consonants, hums that tripped through each

of the known vowels and words that were not, will never be,
words. It doesn't matter how things grew too bright, how fear

etched its haggard lines under the sac of breath in my chest
or how I began to faint before breakfast when my father yelled,

how I'd think he was spinning me around and around, my ankles
bruising against the doorframe, when actually he'd carried me

to the couch, angry again once I'd come to, such a *chickenshit*
I'd fall unconscious to beg off the Orthrus guarding his sympathy. True,

I stole from them, squeezed an entire tube of toothpaste
onto the sofa, shoplifted from the Christian bookstore, kicked

my brother in the *partes*, or as my mother would charily call it,
privates—a word that seemed more than *that*, a promise, a blossom,

a word I'd say to myself over and over. Soon what wide vats,
what lavalieres of words came, faster and blacker, banana leaves

shriveling over flame, canaries set loose in the kitchen, more words
than I could handle bulging darkly from a face I knew,

the tortuous vines of his blood all through me, the fetid and fantastic
blurring from one body to the next—a prowling cat, the cuspids

of splendor seemed to nip at me, needing to hurt. My father's heels
came down like a drunkard's. The wind of his mouth shook doors

all over the world, swung crazily the lanterns near my heart. Long after
the sky snuck from our room, my sister would pet my face. I am

the child, they tell me, who began making things up as soon
as she could speak. We agree he was never drunk—

what we couldn't have said is this: despite what we wish, it's not memory
that tells us who we are but what we find just below the roof

of the body, that precious attic wedged full of words, there
among the ribbons of nightmare, fulgurant eyes, fingers

that shake, shoulders strong and dumb, and the great, insoluble blocks
of love when I look at a photograph of my mother and father

in 1975, three years before my head fell crashingly
through heaven. Who can blame my mother for being so beautiful?

Mother as Opalescent Bottle

Upon falling in love with her, this time in Michigan,
where autumn comes sooner than expected

You sit in the breakfast nook, soundless as the panicle
      of the final red phlox outside the window; you have noticed
small veins beginning to rise over the knuckles and back

of your hand. You are not yet thirty, are not thinking *age*. Once,
      long ago, in church, you sat this way, pressing the veins
of your mother's hand, that web of emerald channels, resilient under

your thumb, pressing down, around, over, like the nose
      of a deer into wild blackberry bush, thinking *this is*, until
your mother's other hand would reach over to still you

and she would nod, slow as the opening tilt of a paper fan,
      toward the preacher. Here, where you are, a glass of water held
as though it were a nuthatch between your knees, the sun's

long, last slant across the back deck, the bowl of chrysanthemums
      dare September to snuff them out and your neighbor's boys
alternate shouting *Die-die-die* with *Ay'ay, Cap'n!* on a trampoline

that yawns them up and snatches them back while they clash
      branches torn from the sagging Sugar Maple. One
of them is crying, voices dissolve as salt in broth but then,

as quickly, begin again. Above them, a black squirrel runs
      the telephone wire with a brilliant yellow ear of corn
in its mouth. All this is part of your mother's body—

that opalescent bottle, that absolute pulchritude, yes, each
      necessary furbelow. You could not find such Latinate words
even if you wanted to, will not, perhaps, until the first snow falls.

Entering the House of Awe

Susanna Childress

Serpentine

After Andrei Rublev's The Savior of Zvenigorod, *15th century*

I.

And when she wakes up, night after night,
her mother takes to holding her at dusk, wrists pinched
with fear, pleading the psalms inside her mouth. Jeremiah

said it first. Spoke straight to her deceitful heart—abrasive
prophet, incisive and unadorned, great cleft of self, damned
truth: above all things, that filthy heart. In the night it dreams

for her. By day, it beats and beats and beats, so that when the music
of years trembles as a human voice, she is no longer afraid
of those bright, black hours. Her fingers pet the yellow pages

of books, petals against her teeth. It is not the nose of Jesus, set
like a pencil upon his face in the tradition of the Greeks. It is
the *muted violet* around his eyes, congealed and weary,

this Jesus. She does not know if he dreamed, who took
to holding him when he woke, and what if he listened for birds
in early morning? How did the lapping Galilee sound?

His small lips, barely rose of gold on that old
parchment, they are closed. Shut lightly, like a pair
of eyes. Or a hand around a stone.

II.

The psalmist told her she could rest on God's shoulders. She is
a lamb, flaccid slab of woman, rinsing out the stains
from her panties in the sink, her body seeping its black scallops

onto strips of fitted cloth. She would tell herself a dream:
holding the cheeks of the Savior of Zvenigorod. Set her mind
on disappearance. Tell her, Isaiah, perfume poured

from that sickening alabaster jar, hands on the Savior's
face, say again, *Comfort, Comfort.* And there is some, shelled out
of a void. The print gives nothing so nicely: says one Russian

art historian, *There is no trace of Byzantine severity. . . .*
She falls asleep to this, arms tucked around herself, Mary
of Magdala, widow of Naim. Each night she has waited

for something to fall, and each morning she wakes, heavy
with mercy, to this damaged fresco of the Christ. A man
found him in a barn, four hundred years after Rublev set him
down. Staring up from the step of a barn, quiet Christ.

III.

How to unfrighten the most frightening affinity. Which
to the small, careening girl, serpentine, her singing mouth,
each rod of earth slipping from her hands. Which to the breasts

that rounded out like a fish's gill with air, the legs and arms
grown long, patience that never did, which to the swiveling neck
on its baluster of vertebrae, to this, and to that, earnest bulbs of light

in the belly, tender folds of the genitals, dreams that helix
hot white: it is not the moustache of Jesus, a line of soil
running into his beard; it is the turning of his face

toward her. Slightly, like a curtain touched with wind. Or the door
an inch from closed. She fears nothing as she fears the loss
of such amity: thank God, his eyes do not search, they do not penetrate.

In Vancouver, You Forgive the American

In Vancouver, you forgive the American next to you at the concert
who watches you. You are no one, yelling songs back
at the singer, craving the kick drum in your knees, your shoulder
bending the organ's pulp, the godforsaken slide guitar. This bloke

standing next to you, his bald head shines. He wants to shout
and shake it too. He needs encouragement. His girlfriend's
boobs have cost money: a red wheelbarrow noses in and out
her cleavage. Taller than Baldie by a Bible, and still your boyfriend's

chin would graze her head. At a chaperoned dance in high school
the Econ teacher told your friend, Watch out for that one,
she's like a bird set loose of its cage. Only, it wasn't true, at all,
it took you years to wear a tank top with straps as thin

as seat belts, which, these days, you recognize is not a tank top
but a *sleeveless blouse*. You didn't become a drunk, don't sell or sleep
till noon. Tonight, you'd considered chocolate underwear in one tiny shop
and, at another, a Buddhist's bracelet urging you to "Leap—"

You're not tattooed, not breasty (of *course*, white *chickens*), and this man
would measure small as you against a stalk of corn. Your boyfriend grows
cucumbers on his veranda, weed in the closets, smiles too often
to scare you, is tall, lean, in love. Your therapist vows

you're nutty but not insane. Therapy is free here. So is this show,
since the gal on stage singing bold as the U.S. flag happens
to be a friend from Birmingham, your let's-drop-kick-this-law-
school friend, who sent you tickets and backstage passes

where by the by you mill about and sip Italian soda, wish you hadn't sweat
so much and maybe read more books. Later, on the patio
of the all-night sushi place, you spy the short bald guy and want
to wave, to offer what you own—a secret: he must take his girl and go

blackberry picking, on the north side, along this road where there's
enough to fill pockets, fill buckets, canyons. You want him
to know where there are berries in this city, that there are berries
here, all September, wild and tangy and dark as a dream.

Halfway to the Jesse James Wax Museum

Marry me, Juliet
is what the billboard says
and though this strikes you as mawkish and/or
ironic in a geeked-out way
suddenly you are crying and none
of the 32 ounces of iced tea will soothe
the feeling it didn't work out
or else it did and whoever Juliet ended up with
was so happy with the message
he's paid or she's paid since anything's possible
to keep it up forever right there
on 44 smack-dab in the middle of Missouri,
one exit before Ft. Leonard Wood/St. Robert

and you've got to wonder how he did it
or she did it since anything's possible only
try as you might you envision someone
named Barry or Nash or Derrick or Tom
+ *Juliet = Luv 4ever*. And actually
it doesn't matter if he took her out
for a steak dinner first or whether she was checking
her teeth and/or complexion in the visor's mirror
and after vacillating he had to snap it shut to say,
"Would you look at that—"
because either way at 70 mph how long would you have
to set your eyes on it and wonder if it was *you*
though there's not so many Juliets in this world

and as you turn to gawk at Barry or Nash or Derrick or Tom
he's grinning but lopsided
like he's peed iced tea in his pants and as for the answer
either way he would've had to pull over,
right? Either way being a reason to hit
the brakes, get off at Ft. Leonard Wood/St. Robert
and do whatever you do when your life
is about to change while you're in the car
which is to say thank God he didn't
get down on his knee
though your fellow did
and it's worked out alright for the two of you,
making the most of clichés

by stepping into them with the bright edge
of laughter at your throats but
since he's got his blue eye mask on
and is trying to sleep has missed
the billboard and can't begin to know
why you're rummaging in the glove department
for a hanky or slurping madly
at the last watery teaspoon of your drink.
"What happened," he'll ask, once, then twice,
and finally insist, "Pull over, lover," only when you do
it's worse than you imagined, so still
when everything else
is moving so fast.

Just like Solomon

It's happening fast, four years unwinding
                            like the tire swing twisted up tight and all of a sudden
            let go, Go on, you tell him,
Take the washer and dryer, take the cat
                        but leave the motorcycle,
        you tell him, I've decided. He doesn't flinch but straight out
says no. No, he says, it's mine. This
                            might stun you, only
        it doesn't, same as your bleached-hot hair
                        didn't stun him at the DMV
when you changed titles, when he said, Halve a thing, see if you don't feel
        full of wrong. You want to say,
                            What's it matter when, after hating him
for so long, I can't get Merle Haggard
                            out of my damn head? You
            hold onto the sounds of this inside your mouth, the way
you don't let much of anything shrink away these days
                            though it goes and goes
            whether you like it or not: shock,
                            the blotched red couch, his mother
that first Thanksgiving taking your picture over and over—You two,
        she kept on saying, You two,
                            with her camera clicking and this
you've clutched so hard it tastes like a nickel
                            under your tongue, though right now
            all you taste is misery so you take the bike keys
and throw them straight at his eyeballs
                            and you both stand still and
            just when you think for sure he'll whip off his hat, slap
his knee and yell your name, he says, calm as pie, I hope you
        find somebody, somebody who'll be
                            good to you and give you
a baby, and then he says he *means* it and comes just close enough
        to rub a knuckle under your chin
                            and then he's pulling at the dryer,
fooling with that stupid metal coil that breaks
                    if you touch it wrong, but he doesn't touch it wrong
                            and it doesn't break and this
is the dark almond lodged in your throat when you remember
        what you said once: if I have to
                            I'll saw the place in half,
        I swear I will.

Entering the House of Awe

Susanna Childress

What Lingers

As pitiful as a diver
far out in Suma Bay
who has lost an oar from her boat,
this body
with no one to turn to.
—Ono No Komachi *(834-?)*

If it's not her own body, she'll
push it away, slowly, the summer-heavy sweat a gracious film
against her neck. If it is her body, she'll bring it back
from its surrendered countries, back
to her unwitting command: hand, shoulder, hip, dim stalk of thigh,
second hand. There—distant ankles. From the stretch
of swollen hours, dark, sap-fingered,
circus-hot, she lets what lingers name her, fall away, morning poignant
as the tall cat-tail perched against its lonesome cup.
                                                    Today, again,
it is her own body. Somewhere reckless
within her, as she runs her palms over the chapped tips
of elbows, vaguely hairless arms, as she reaches
into the shapes of anxious sun above her bed,
she wants his body there, if to pull
away from, to untangle in a solid, unlikely way, letting
what lingers from another frog-sung July
name her whole soft, stupid body, name his, a living beast
who dreams, wind, mud-speckled, eye-green.

Fetching

1.

Coming home, her flight's delayed two hours, and when she arrives
       at the farmhouse on Papermill Road the first thing she sets eyes on
in the dim light is a note taped to the mailbox: *Could you please*
       put mail in the box bellow until the birds are done?

For minutes she tries to recall what a *box bellow* might be—
       another miscellaneous crib, speckled with dried kernels of corn,
something her grandmother has upended and dusted. She notices
       envelopes jutting from a cardboard box on the ground *below*

until the birds are done. She creaks wide the mailbox door to find
a swirl of grasses and twigs, ragweed root and a tatter of blue ribbon.

2.

Great-Grandma Olive boiled half a dozen eggs for Mother
       to take on the plane to California, where she would meet
Father's family and show them the white gold ring he bought
       by preaching a whole summer of Sundays for the Baptists.

Olive had never been on a plane. In fact, she had not been
       out of Indiana since '79, when a horse show across the river
drew her into Kentucky for the first time in a decade. Even then
       she would not let go her bulky, quilted purse, its pockets hiding pieces

of taffy wrapped in wax paper, a family joke almost as old as she,
born two weeks before the grand and tidy burst of 1900.

3.

The Chardells tell it that Great-Aunt Gwen was betrothed
       before she knew what her father had done, 17 and reading books
a woman usually didn't: Emerson, for one. So when she went in a calico dress
       to Seth Ferguson and begged he take back the tobacco fields from her daddy

and forget the whole thing, that she was in love with Jesse Chardell till she died,
       she didn't know such a kindred thing as love had taken hold, too, of Seth,
that he'd cry that day, wiping his big hands on his britches, and declare
       he loved her so hard he'd pay for her and Jesse's wedding

if that would truly make her happy. This is what they tell you, the britches,
    the calico dress, never mentioning if happiness is what she got
and each year the pink blooms on the tobacco plants curl up just before July
    and the whippoorwill scoops up fat yellow worms from the leaves.

        4.

She was seven years old when they told her her mother had been killed.
    It took another seven for Grandma to tell her how it happened,
the sharp discs of the combine and Mother and Daddy up top, hauling out
    errant stalks of corn long as their legs. They'd guess she got dizzy

or maybe was looking off to the pasture, or even, though this is her daughter's
    rendition entirely, had craned her neck to make out the pale half-egg
of harvest moon, turning too quick to direct Father's gaze
    in the afternoon sky, and she fell in. For years they've told her brother

it wasn't his fault, that first summer Thom managed the wheel, though these days
    it's whiskey Thom listens to and the prickly sweat of memory,
knowing Father will no longer come for him in the cool haze of the bar,
    shoulder him up, lay him down in the bed of the Ford to sleep it off.

        5.

The Dupont Hornets are raising money for the school library,
    and when she settles on the carrot cake muffins instead of Pamela's
mince meat pie, it hurts the woman's feelings. *Nice of you to come back,*
    Pam says, palming her quarters. *Nice to be back,* she says, the muffins

wobbling on the paper plate. *There's some people,* Pam says, *who know
    how a fancy thing goes sour. Yes,* she says slowly, unsure if Pam means
her schooling or her marriage. *Yes,* Pam says again, *Some people think this place
    is all crops and hogs and crossroads.* She stares at a daub of icing on her thumb,

but it's chicory she tastes at the back of her mouth. When she looks up, Pam
seems sorry. *Your daddy was a fine preacher,* Pam says, *Help yourself to a little lemonade.*

6.

The year they drew her mother's body from under the combine,
        she watched her father tear down the wall between kitchen and dining room.
In the rubble he found a newspaper from 1884, a matchstick airplane with one
        wing, and a handful of buffalo nickels. He stared at the newspaper a long time,

as if he remembered its stories, and he stuck it in the back of his Bible
        with the leather cover worn smooth as a sorrel's neck, his name in the corner
so faded you could just make out the anglicized consonants.
        He and Thom worked to rebuild the rooms that summer,

Thom never speaking of the woman he thought he destroyed, Father unable
to stop speaking of her, of the moon, of Isaiah, who promised *comfort*.

7.

If she has learned to take a place seriously, its Muskatatuck Park,
        just north of the Ohio River, cuddled in the outskirts of Jennings County.
No one had to tell her its mute, sacred places under pine and willow,
        the old stories of Susquehanna and Cherokee, even older stories, glaciers

that rippled southern Indiana like a woman shaking out a tablecloth.
        Here she met shy Eddie Chardell, who came to Muskatatuck in the evenings
to look for the coming winter, striped caterpillars and roots of wild chives
        touched with orange. He never asked why she came, and if he had,

she wouldn't have known what to tell him, something of her mother, perhaps,
        or Great-Grandma Olive, both of whom she was having trouble remembering.
The second time they met, Eddie brought Longfellow, butternut squash,
        and her very first beer. His voice dipped low and foretold an unkind winter.

8.

Her grandmother is the most reticent storyteller in the county. She
        is the kind of woman who wrote her granddaughter a letter
each month she was away, relaying, *My beans are about*
        ———— *yea long* and *You ought to see the forsythia today,*

it would stop your breath up short. In the twenty-two years between her mother's
      and father's deaths, she never saw her grandmother cry,
though the tremor to her bottom lip has been there as long as she can recall
      and shadows under the eyes, so violet she'd always wanted

to reach up and touch them and to ask what she shouldn't: why water arches
      from the hose like a rope, why the eggs are flecked with blood,
if it hurts to get old, or alone. The woman's told her enough, though, the way
      telling, fashioned like a nest, is not the sound of a thing but its hearth.

     9.

Aphids gather on the porch today, the hard rain calling them up
      from the ground. She tries to sketch the fence twined with honeysuckle,
the heifer from memory, blank-eyed and sweet-milked, but she's tired
      of flowers and roots, weed and fern, the bovine. Today she wants the angry

call of a jaybird, a cup to fall and break (*pucha!*), the rain and the stink of wood smoke.
      She drops to her knees and frowns at the aphids, their gridded anterior
nimbly making a path along the steps. She's fetched today: a dweller
      in the bewildering land of the mind, not unlike Indiana, its cavities

and its coils of light, its stones and minnows, its hovering moon
a promise of God's, something like nectar, something like thirst.

Architecture of an Apology

When you see each other again   this time under the pretext
of an apology he wants to make   in a hallway   after the plenary speaker

his wife stands there trying not to look uncomfortable   which at the moment is
impossible and gets you feeling sorrier for her than for yourself   a particular
accomplishment   considering inside your coat pocket   two fingers

pinch a balled-up gum wrapper like it's your cherry stone of a brain and this means
you're each sorry for something now   you   for her and she for him and he for

what?   mislabeling love is what you're guessing though in the actual air his
        Sorry   doesn't carry like you'd imagined   the lam of a beefy helicopter
and of course   now that you're standing here and now that he's said his apology

you can't for the life of you figure how to respond   this gulch between your mouth
and the long tunnel   to his ticker   *Me too* isn't what you mean at all

and *I forgive you*   also sounds wrong though it's closer to what   belongs
in the space he's cleared   between you   What you manage
       is *Thank you*   the one thing left on that short list of possibilities

but when he says *I'm just tired* *of being pissed off*   it's not hard to fill in
at you   and you could gasp   like you'd been smacked but he   with more curls

and paunch than you remember   is the one gathering up a raw breath as though
        it feels right to say these things to the woman he   didn't marry
for which you have shouted at the moon—God's good eye—so many

thanks   and for whatever reason   the whole sweet speech you prepared
this morning   as you brushed your teeth   has started to slip away

Words just   drop their napkins on their plates   and saunter out the house
so all you can do is nod dumbly that   Certainly   *Being pissed off is a waste*
of energy   What it seems   is that his apology has made a strange

shape   of your throat   you're guessing a triangle with too much   susurration
say   *Isosceles*   and now the tiny pellet of gum wrapper has lodged itself beneath

a fingernail   like the hard angles of your youthful mistakes   his   and yours
each   of us   so ridiculous   we thought the house we built of cones   would stand
in the forest forever and by now   you're ready to leave but can't quite make it

happen   unsure how to construct   a salutation for him or his wife   who was also
     your friend once   and who   this whole time has been inspecting the wiry flex
of her wrist   one hand rotating back and forth like the smallest   nodding head

The Boiled Clean Feel of Your Bones

In the middle of your floor, a man is crying.
                                    You are on top of him,
   trying to kiss his shoulder,
                       to hold still the corners of his face, perched
in dereliction, a skin of remorse balancing itself
    carefully over bones,
                     the absurd cylindrical hope
of bones, sturdy and pillaged, as they are,
     at once.
              His face is beautiful, his face hates you,
                    the bric-a-brac of usage, the doors
opening and shutting on the tongue,
                             its dumb oil, and now
      you finger the cracked peppercorn
                               of that-which-is-not-but
   ache hanging in your room, so you pull your hips
away from him and the particles
                    of your bodies melt from each other,
    that river of borrowed blood, the enterprising cells.
    Now, having emptied
                 its dark pockets, air falls
        from the four tines of the ceiling fan,
                         the unbelievable,
stupid ceiling fan, its slow spin the only perfection you can think of,
from here, on your back, in your room.
                      Sometimes,
   your lips making a strange bargain, *I can feel you break.*
                         He offers
nothing yet, the rhythm of sorrow so coarse
it holds tantamount distance
                from psyche to Now, spirit to Yes, body
to God. *I can't pray like this*, he says, his voice a shallow pit,
                      Look at me,
       and the angles of his face
                  are an uncatched latch
    at the spruce wood gate. *I want to pray,* he tells you,
  but you realize
       it's not him speaking, not him
after all—it's you, who knows that the black shape
                    in the corner

is the wicker basket, filled today with towels
                              and a lavender sachet,
    you who knows the boiled clean feel
                              of your bones, *I want to cry out—*

The Hyssop Tub

Then, as Thy self to leapers hast assignd
With hyssop, Lord, thy Hyssop purg me so
And that shall cleanse the Leapry of my mind
Make over me Thy mercys streams to flow
So shall my whitness scorn the whitest snow
  To eare and heart send sounds and thoughts of gladness
  That bruised bones may dance away their sadness.

— "Psalm 51, *Miserere mei Deus,*" Mary Sidney, *The Sidney Psalter*

I.

Great harridan of my heart   who is to say

you knew anything at all   Once   I bargained

with a man the whole night long to call   what thing hung

between us *love*   as though by scraping the rough

from a coconut   it could be   a carrot   I thought

I understood how much I hated   myself   It is not

easy to see the peony hang its scented head   No

    I willed the petals fall   my palm   almost

full of unassuming   gloaming pink   an occasional

ant across my stem of a wrist   What

I could not see   I knew   I could not see   What

woman   believes she has the turrets   of God

beneath her rattlebox of skin   The flag   I flew

for so long read   *I'll erase myself if you want me to*

II.

Let them have the dancers. I'm in love with the woman in *Le Tub*,
her russet sponge and russet hair. Russet jar delicate as a teapot, filled,
I want to imagine, with the oils of gardenia, some flower from the family
of Rubiaceae, not the bitter leaves of Labiatae. She is a careful
woman, russet yarn between her needles on the counter. You, too,
loved her, I can tell. It would have been easy with each hatchmark to deliquesce
her body with water but you did not give a glistening—you gave the tub,
simple iron sphere, opening up and out, and the sempiternal
turning of her head, her body dry, ginger-ashen, like someone crouching
to kiss a new land, saying *Praise be*, saying *I believed*, and the crepuscular small
of her back knows how what is poured over her shoulders from the mouth
of the splotched pitcher will rivulet. I see the hairbrush within reach, the towel.
Later, semi-submerged in bronze she practices the Portuguese she knows,
grips an instep, the tub's rim, O Degas. She asks over and again *Como ser limpo?*

III.

My father is the woman in the striped dress, her hand holding my waist
tender as an oblong bread. My mother is the woman with her right hand
rinsing my foot in the bowl. My beloved is the woman leaning into
the child who knows her lap like a honey possum's marsupium: their heads
so circular, everything asymmetrical, even the cholera they wash away. Degas
befriended Cassatt, both who imitated the bathing women of Japanese ukiyo-e
prints at the Ecole des Beaux-Arts. It has nothing to do with me, but now
one of Cassatt's few nudes, just this one—is me. Do you understand? I am *Woman
Bathing*, not   safe as *The Bath*, my striped dress   unbuttoned   to the waist
my back   etched carefully as the pitcher on the roiling carpet. The tiniest
glimpse of water in the tub's an avatar. She   the miraculous drafts(wo)man
said the medium made her do it   said *drawing on a plate requires   strict control
as the surface   mercilessly retains every mark*   See   what marks   remain
   the clean lines   of my nebbish back   the undoing of   my stains

IV.

For each of the years I was *perdido* as a pebble   in the basalt

of lithosphere   it was not which Caravaggisti I liked best

but whose brutal themes   I   could bear   not Gentileschi's Judith

or Ribera's Bartholomew   but for early Velázquez I was so

entranced   with his Seville water carrier   ripped sleeve   swarthy

forehead   the goblet of water   the shadowy hand   the russet

poncho   How could I have missed   the russet

poncho Who   could save me from loving   the droplets of water

on the earthen jug   from thinking Diego   give me

       this *genre scene*   the plebeian   like me

every time   you give   his ancient body   beside the boy

who stares at the rend   in the sleeve   he will take   the goblet

and drink what the carrier brought on his shoulder to them

like a constellation   sloshing toward   Bethlehem

V.

It was Bathsheba   on the roof in the tub   but David who pleaded

       Cleanse me with hyssop and I will be   clean

Bathsheba   whose name I remembered   because

of the tub when I was not old enough to understand   what

the King wanted of her   BATHSHEBA   we call to you

centuries of women who both   knew and didn't know

better   Believe me   your voice   had you had one to speak

in holy text   is mine is the Black-Throated Green Warbler's

   whose song even without words sounds   wanting

I know what you wanted   I hope as much as the aspergillus twig

shaken for purification   I hope   he loved you

as someone has begun   to love me   When we're apart

he says *Put your hand close to your face* he says   *Your fingers brushing*

your forehead   Your palm   hovering your mouth   It's me

VI.

Mary Mary Countess   of Pembroke sister of the Queen's fallen one   you
proffered this *translation*   this *paraphrase*   lines that perhaps
as you had   Laura   speak through   Petrarch   you give this woman
something   of her own   (the male Black-Throated Green Warbler
has been known to sing   466 songs   in one hour   to call a mate) for
it is not   *let the bones you have crushed   rejoice* but   *that bruised bones   may*
dance away   their sadness   It is after all   to lepers God has been
assigned   their purging   part cedar wood   part crimson yarn pair
of doves   hyssop   Rabbinic commentary offers *You   were proud*
like the cedar and the Holy One   Blessed be He   humbled you
like   this hyssop that   is crushed   by everyone   At the crucifixion
I lifted   a sponge of vinegared wine on a branch of hyssop   So
who's up for being ground   like mint or white sage   What's   the chance
you take   to give   only and not   only   then   we dance

VII.

June's last   rainstorm   a jay
                    perches on the ledge   beneath our roof
                          to wait the entire   heady
               shower out   I too sit here   and think
the roof could stand
                    for anything   but the ledge
the ledge is definitely you   Josué   and now that I have come to this
          I must   finish it   I am not   the blue jay
          at all

       I am
the rain   Given this

                          tell me

               how could the bird in the cove
       be   anything but   our love

II.

And in the days
when you find yourself orphaned,
emptied
of all wind-singing, of light,
the pieces of cursed bread on your tongue,

may there come back to you
a voice,
spectral, calling you
sister!
from everything that dies.

—Galway Kinnell, "Under the Maud Moon"

Chloé Phones after Three Weeks Working at the Home

It's crazy   she says   I can count on my nostrils who *hasn't* been abused here molested
tormented   scarred in some way   Some throw their shoes and scream   some know
how to wield a knife   one cut off the ear   of his cat   Little Shop of Disorders   she
calls it laughing that thrown laugh   one forced an eight-year-old into sex   but *his*
mom's a multiple who named him   Caroline after one of her selves   You can't say
"crazy" here is the thing— someone   undoubtedly is and Madison's mother must've
cussed to a group of women as in *Life's a bitch   ladies*   When angry   this child
yells   *Bitchladies Stupid bitchladies*   Madison who can't bathe by herself
having been raped by her stepfather   How about "That's nuts" No   no good
"Insane" Worse   "Wacky"   Well   then scalded in a bath   when he panicked
scrubbing at the spread of blood between her legs   I've got it   "That's wild"
Another Maddy-ism   she says   is *I already did a* shitloaf *of spelling words*   and
There's a shitloaf *of dishes   ain't there* That's wild she tries   that's wild   It'll
work she says but isn't satisfied I can tell It's the way she laughs   hot   stippled
There needs to be no right word   There needs to be a wide hole   a
whole mouth   where the right word   isn't

Sōlus Meets Ipse

& this, this is me not writing the *typical American anecdote*. Here I am not contemplating my navel (or, novel, that too will work), not wandering into jazz bars, not lighting up, not staying all night. This is me not moustaching a picture of the Pope to scandalize my aunties, not falling in ecstatic love with my breasts & wearing them down—& while I'm at it, this is me not calling the penis a blind worm. Look at me, not pillow-booking, not on my anglo-angst, his afro-angst, not whining like a capricious country hit single over my cancerous parakeet, botched Jell-O, the Reds, energy-saving light bulbs, frigid neighbors, pollen allergies. What if, by heaven, I wrote of famine or genocide, the man made quadriplegic when his children pushed him out a window, the teenager raped by her math teacher, but the truth is that I don't know where Serbia is. Who does, really? The Canadian fellow, fat enough for three of us, looking at my poems—his editor in Bosnia (*Have you heard of it?*) relays a story of sheikhs floating on a river between the two countries. Barry, you're right. Barry, this is me not knowing where to go from here, having nothing but an American anecdote to write, & oh, O! having wandered deeper into that— lost, stuck, dumb.

Torn

Recently a friend admitted his fear of birds, how
    as a child he'd meant to rescue a fallen robin,
                had reached up
  to return the bird when a grey sprawl of lice
            left its body
    and scattered on his hand, so he dropped the bird and ran.
                It made me
      think of you, the way a grown man relives
his ancient anxieties more vividly with time—that field
    of sorghum stretching before my friend
              like the rest of his life, each
white cedar humming under its scabs of bark,
          branches promising
  oriel, blackbird, grackle as he flapped the lice from his arm.
             It may
    be true, that even the smallest deaths are mother
to beauty, but you spared your children stories of their grandparents launching
    plates at each other, of LA gang fights,
          you traded your buddy's
  blown-off face in Nha Trang for the kneaded silence of its truth
    beneath your red red *sangre*:
           you knew what it was to fear,
             you let me
  believe man is good, the four chambers of the heart
    more like a cow's prodigious stomachs than the cavities
of a pistol.
    I crawled beneath your knees to watch
    cop shows on TV,
      hollered my long midnights
when the closet kicked with deer,
      the woman's ears bled bees,
        the neighbor boy
  clamped his penis against my cheekbone at someone's
    birthday while upstairs they pinned the tail on the donkey—
green and blue balloons floated down, popped
      at his elbows. My friend says,
A bird's most terrifying
      feature is its tongue—blanched, cracked—think of it
  coming straight for your face.

I mean to laugh
a little, his arms raised, fingers aimed at my eyes
like claws.
         Instead I hear myself gasp, as though I could begin
         to understand this, his personal horror.
                                        I cannot. I think

of Philomela—human turned nightingale
              whose tongue, torn ragged like the kitchen curtain,
continued to sing.
         Papi, how could you know that balloons,
                                     to this day, loose
my bowels? I never told you.
              I swore it was a dream.

Where Wings Could Be

Preserve not, want not. If the tumbleweed of faith
kept its spore, as my ear its shape,

rumpled evenly as a nest, no wind would send me
reeling. Send me reeling. What's left of the glass pitcher

from Denmark, a wedding present four months old,
is the handle. The rest sounded resolutely, shards swept

singing to the dustpan, his shoulders keeping
time with the broom, me in the doorway, stepped back

to lament elbow, glass, one movement's vacuum
of grace knocking all beauty to the floor.   What I need

from life: a few loves brilliant with return. Bundle
of papers, music, each pocked round of opportunity/ mistake/

accolade/ what have you, a proof, here and there, knowing
the nothingness of knowing: the self a dim understanding,

those great hollow spots where wings could be: brutal,
stunning flight.   O Daedalus. O inescapable

God. Air, lungs, legs and belly, holy holy torpid heat:
holy tubes, holy rigor. My father stretched on the harness

his therapist swears will soothe seven bulging, two ruptured
discs, my father who answers *How are you feeling* with

With my hands, who has slept on the floor
for years holy   disc holy nest   sac toponym and cup.

Saucer. Diastole. Sweet systole. One holiness spread
across all faces, one stroke from the fingers

of truth: what of the body is left to sing? Maybe
feathers. Maybe not. Even they are gift—hen, pheasant,

mallard. I said, send me reeling. México for the preacher
electrocuted during baptismal. California

for the baby girl suffocated by a fallen window fan,
Oklahoma's mother of four run over right in front

of her kids and even the man who strung himself up in BC
and his wife returning a box of ashes to South Africa,

Lord. What I need from time to time: not news;
reverie. Should I beg my daily bread or sun and shield?   Once

small as a fawn I slept in the curl of my father's arm,
held in that holding pattern we know as love and soon

I was grown and soon a mandolin and soon opalesque,
a handle unattached from its cylinder and spout, desolate

with what I couldn't name, a particular ache I sent on up
to Jesus for our set-on-a-spindle globe, for the undone,

the millions. For the breaching heads of Calla lilies
fallen from their stems in my father's back. Send me,

send me. In winter all but basil in the nook of the great oak
will yield. In spring the knots of faith trip up the spine

into the neck, shoot straight to that patchwork of nervous gray
matter and what brain can hold, dear God, such soft   pelt.

In the Pocket of Your Winter Coat

It frightens you, what you think
you don't deserve, all of us standing around shouting
Happy Birthday Dear Da-ad—
you're plagued with a tart humility when I'm the kind
who wants everyone to kiss my face, sing, buzz, eat
their whole hearts out for me.   Which is not

altogether true: last time I was the center of attention,
a joke I made too long, had to finish off
with something not originally part of the joke
at all, I was winded with delight to receive their laughter. Around
the edges it terrified me,   their faces saying
Thank you, their hands in their laps

and come to think of it there's something
about admiration that almost hurts, which is to say,
that joke wasn't some miracle, was waiting there, like a wad
of money in a jacket packed away, like all the capsules and nooks
of ourselves we don't quite know as extant—
quirk and dream,   flower stems,   balustrade. If it

can happen, this may be how we spoon
the thick soup of our love: one unknown place after another
shoring up within us, shouldering that which comes, say,
your child, one who taunts and charms, raw
          as an artichoke, working her way into jocularity
and your finest rage. When she starts to pull down

the sky, separating stars like halves of bread, locates her heart and it,
too, is a red planet, when the two of you fumble at last
to a broken knowing of each other, as perhaps
father and daughter must,   she'll recall you
spraying down steel chicken feeders with your thumb
over the mouth of the hose, flicking your wrist and fingers

after a drawn-out anecdote like the Filipinos who taught you songs in Ilocano,
cupping Roger's cheek on the porch
where every Sunday he confessed to gambling, bringing
bottles of Coca-Cola to her polished-apple face among

the junior high cheerleaders who were not washing so much as splashing
cars, and that once,   catching her in a strange, crafted lie—

how she's unable to see the chalkboard. She will,
in fact, recollect the kerosene stove
sputtering, the way you sat her down on the old
sofa after the optometrist's telling diagnosis
and showed her with alarming calm the bottom
of your shoe.   If indeed it's *celebration* you're forced

to reconsider the spring of your sixth decade, let it be
the way a girl   will watch your face during thunderstorms
or veer gleefully from the hallowed punch lines
to which neither of you can stick (Papi, let's live inside this one: What
did the Buddhist say to the hot dog vendor? Make me
        one with everything.) Should you remember

the tatty couch, a sullen celery-green,   she sat
the long while till you said, soft as a song on the radio, *I needed
a new pair of shoes*, your fingers flapping a bald sole,
        but you needed glasses. And when you stood
and walked away, you left everything: her own
great, blank, brazen stupidity, the awful mercy

she could not parse out. Your knowing exactly how to love her
was no miracle, no fluke or trick,   it was you
palming something staid and weightless
in the pocket of your winter coat, the navy one
with duct-tape on its sleeve: there in the pouch of corduroy,
knuckled-thin, a blooming wad of dollars.

A Note to Martin Luther King, Jr. Regarding the Use of Certain Transitive and Intransitive Verbs

Sir, when I came home quoting *nearly* every line
of that lambent speech, played on Mrs. Dowell's beat-up
tape recorder during afternoons the autumn of my thirteenth
year, my father explained to me your (a new word)

infidelities. Here, in the capital of Texas, on this grand
old campus, your academic robe billows in cast iron
to spite the old aspersion, the features of your face speak
as much as, against your immobile head,

the pearl-clouded sky. I am a girl from the hills, white as bone,
and if I am honest I'll admit the one snatch of that pavid set
of junior-high courses I still recall: *With this faith we will be able*
to hew out of the mountain of despair a stone of hope. Is it true

more American streets are named after you than any other
figure in our tricky history? Which is what reminds me,
your literal figure on my walk to school each day,
past the four-story LBJ museum and the towering

music hall, past the fountain which sprays so much so high
that its water, upon return, hits the walk like a body, past
folks who send Frisbees soaring into October, to, finally,
you, quiet monolith—I didn't care that day if you'd made

babies with women besides your wife. I'm older
now, Dr. King, can recognize the way I cleave, I hew: you
are not my father, whom I love, the mountain I yen
to carve myself out of into a hard, dark pebble of *dream*.

Love, Anonymous

It used to be, back in the ninth grade swirl of skirts and books,
a vacant look on every boy's face but Ricky Kearns who
swears he saw your panties on his way up the stairs,
you dreamed of the kind of attention only you
could give yourself, so much, in fact, you'd tape anonymous notes
to your locker on Valentine's Day, dangle a pouch of candies
on the latch to make your point. *Do you know*, one note began,
*you've the wit of a pasquinade, the mind of a Cubist, the sad strength
of a eunuch and oh my darling, the quick song of a finch at roost.* All this
and Tootsie Rolls too. *Love, Anonymous.* Someone's got it bad
for you, and after class when your friend saunters close to speculate who,
you know she knows, enough of the wisp
on the ends of *h*s to give you away; she's too kind to say, takes
the Jolly Ranchers you proffer in a kind of détente: *It's true,
you want to squawk, surely this fella's right about me?* Now,

                                                  years after you gave it up

and instead let your sister buy you the Future Farmers'
stupid carnations each Valentine's Day so you know
how *awesome* you are, *chica!*—now that someone has left a true
anonymous gift for you in the mailroom/lounge, a square orange
box of sweets—it bothers you. You're unsure how to be
grateful, grinning dumb as a sock monkey at each colleague who checks
the shelf of cubbies—unnerved, your tongue pinked
with candy, a small light signaling inside you, like the last shriek
of a slow train, the pilfered work of *cherish* or *maybe*
or *saccharify.* When you tell your mother, your sister, you won't mention
how you left the box under your name for four days
in case someone had made a mistake. Or this: in the blank loam
of unknowing, a nugget of fear, a tiny moment opened
roughly as a stolen purse. Who knew yearning's spurn
was proximity? Here you are, inured to white space,

                                                  waiting the scrawl of a lover.

The Necessary Dark

I send the letter, in the corner a stamp
like the eye of a fish, promising something

neither of us know how to say. I send the rain, the cracked
green shell of a tortoise, the top loop of scissors your thumb

slides into. The last letter you sent unfolds like an accordion:
so you're standing at the sink, scrubbing tomatoes, sharpening

a knife and the problems keep coming, though it is what
you know you must do, teaching sixth graders in a time of war

all you know of love: this one stayed after to learn his parts
of speech, this one knows a word—*fagged*—you must explain

even to adults. Under a rhythm of longing like July's dream of gourds
and beetles, here I am, a good piece already spooned from the cup

of my heart, that hickory meat, that red-breasted bird. Indirection,
you say, protects us from truths we cannot bear. You, gentle

as a mandolin, are right, and I will know when to say
what I mean to say. Until then, I send both hands

into the whorl of my hair, where I find a bee, flowers' syrup
on its legs, which I also send, which will not be

enough. If Rilke, too, is right, beauty a terror that never crushes
but comes close, we have whole margins of hope, will call that part

of the day exactly what it is, the necessary dark, left for me
to find like a vial deep inside a cabinet, the farmer's mark

on the flank of a ram, you at the kitchen counter, you
at the desk. I send to your emptied mouth a whistle

on the end of a string, my last true place, silence plaited
in the gristle of the spine and tendons of the arms raised waist-high,

hollowed out as if to hold you, yes, even this I send.

Instructions for the Twitterpated, Nightingaled, and Sore in Love

Begin by throwing something away: the microwave,
for example.   This will be easier after the crimson hibiscus
fall from where you hung them to dry, their huge corolla spilled
like dark tortillas and your own ticking pulse

won't stop you from sagging to the floor with a heady,
comprehensive loss, those flowers you strung up by the broom
stunningly ruined, their long stems, too, snapped like the legs
of a praying mantis.   After this, sweep your arm

across the cupboards and fill a canvas sack with the butter pickles
and wheat germ nobody bothered to open, the prize-winning box
of cereal, the spindled cheese grate.   Whatever you do, do not
toss the egg shells, which, after having broken each open,

you returned to the carton like a dozen viscous sockets
that might yet sing.   Run your fingers over their fractured edges
and don't be surprised if you've never touched
such a thing, parchment-thin, specked with the memory of locust,

millet, wind, now crooked halves of a yolky hollow,
cupped grottos of sound you've become deaf to, ears dwarfed
with your own importance—*to thy high requiem become a sod*—
so that when you're standing here with me, wondering

what you'll do without the toaster oven and why my face
is an insouciant cheddar pink, you must offer the old knife with one hand
and arch my back with the other.   Watch me slice open two avocados
and with palpable shock behold their pits, so beautiful

that after you leapfrog the gates of heaven and get a good look
at God's knuckles it's these you'll recall, not the trash bin,
not the emptied palms, goose bumped with secret.   For now,
stand still a decent while: turn your hand over, let them go.

Weaving

These ribbons—the thin, falling strings—are meant for her hands. This
is why she has long hair. He's begun to think it entertains her,

separating the rivers as she does, the straight, deep brown a thousand paths,
of her going on and on with her fingers in her hair, restless, tired,

and the truth is he's tired too, head in her lap, nearly dreaming
of the two of them, right here, a facsimile of what is,

her knuckles lost in her hair, fascinated with the slip and pull of both
her hands in the shadow hanging from her head. He means

to try out the word as she would say it, *pelo*. Instead he imagines the word
in her voice, the cords of her throat offering sounds he cannot. She takes

a drink of morning juice and he opens his eyes in time to see
a fine strand of saliva swing between the cup and her mouth

before it pops into nothingness, the soft air skimming every thing,
the daylight his friend for a moment, backlighting that subtle wing

of spit. He reaches up, an awkward stretch for his shoulder, presses
his fingertips along her face. Yesterday he saw a blackbird flying

low to the ground, trailing a long dark string, moving fast, weaving,
skittish, away from the other birds. There was something

brave about it, that nut-sized aggression: *I will make a home.*
From the middles of her fingers, he untangles her hair.

All Hallow Even

Though we knew each other
without overlapping
our clothes,
still, with this autumn wind's sound,
I find myself waiting for you.
—Izumi Shikibu *(974-1034)*

The night most of America snapped on
black capes and gauzy era-imitation dresses, our hostess
bearing her torso-length cleavage in a jumpsuit the color

of a spinach tortilla, you tell me you love me.   You say it leaning
on the car, two blocks from the house strumpeting its music,
and though I believe you, I can't quite shake my need
to question where the festivity ends and you begin, so

here I stand, quivering in a kimono, parsing out
the beaded length of your announcement.   Tonight, for the first time,
I saw you dance like a drunkard, which was the clearest example

yet of your undeclared love since you were not drunk and *do not*
dance. Since I'm greater parts Pollyanna than Zelda Fitzgerald: you up
and decide I need to laugh, no one else dancing, not even
Magic Genie, who gripped my elbow till you returned

with your Whiskey Sour and he sauntered away smiling
like a wine stain, enormous blue bulb of his hat
clocking people in the face left and right, and your friends telling me

how fantastic you are, kind, articulate, *A catch* is what
the woman said and her husband winked at me as if we'd grown up together
though we just met in the master bathroom where we took refuge
from the man with a tray of triangled sandwiches

surrounding a foot-long rubber penis or the other guy
with gigantic strap-on boobs looming over cocktails, a lady
in one of those sexy bunny outfits offering, *Mine are real*, flickering

with laughter and toggling his plastic nipples while her tail
shook and shook to the music—but when you danced,
sharper than Brando in the only suit you own, it was the outlandish
waggle of your neck, your eyes snapping open

like bean pods, your palms shimmying up as if to request
what you cannot sound out, *perdón, pelo, pequeñina*, what is louder
than each song pounding its *loves* and *wants*—   I know who you are,

peanut candy dissolving in my mouth and your two hands reaching
for my face, I know exactly who you are, your whole self,
stop-sign tall, eyes flecked green, how your hot spirit
seems to bob each moment like a hard-boiled egg.   Here, the dark

bolder than that costume with the crotch cut out, I may understand
what Anne Morrow wrote in her diary while falling
for Charles Lindbergh, "All my life, in fact, my world—my little

embroidery beribboned world—is smashed," which might be
the least romantic thing to say about a man who truly knew the wind
from the whirl, but the most enchanting, too; those others swept aside,
"all the pseudointellectuals," she wrote, "the sophisticates, the posers,"

and this is how it might be, our worlds shattered with a clarity
we don't know what to do with, separating
somehow the festival of human desire, that exquisite

house, its exquisite owners, their Japanese herb gardens
and martini menu and Who's-Who I would have wilted into
but for you, man who brushes my hair, who
shapes lanterns from paper, who presses against

the window of a life that, as Wendell Berry has it, *won't compute*: love,
work for nothing, spot the field where we'll lay beneath
an old tree, and say to the most piano part of my ear: *Look, there.*

Of Course I Hit at the Moon

The summer I learned what it meant to writhe, sent
        firecracking, spiraling up the human tendril but stopping short
of penetration, climax dropping away like a torch
        down a well, I also learned the timely pulse of dawn,
tangled in sheets at 5 am, unable to sleep in that state
        of the body, undiffused, the sun balancing dark and streak
of light. Somehow, in the unshattered center, a strange
        satisfaction lifted up, mute as an early morning
on my mother's back porch, shelling peas before the heat set in,
        cows mulling behind the electric fence, hyssop and June bugs
wet with dew: I had not given yet my gift, though even I
        did not know it as such, could not have guessed its bright
weight, like a burst of carnival sounds, its gaudy strength,
        spun high, sky-stark as a Ferris wheel carriage. Of course

it scared me, stuck inside as a tree holding back its spring leaves.
        Of course I hit at the moon with my body's round fury,
those seasonal limbs opening and closing. Friends said
        they respected this, my *holding out*, but their sidelong glances
laughed a little. Summers later, it doesn't matter
        who was right, for I learn a lesson to shock the blood
and beans of my ridiculous body, like a sock of marbles
        sent knocking on a glass bowl. Heavy with our dumb
sure love, so rooted by that conifer I tremulously climb, *marriage*, having
        discovered the most arcane part of myself, struck flat
with its thrashed breaching each time, the bearer of such largess:
        delirium, you gifting with me, reckless, in and out of the only
earth we know for whole minutes—afterwards, as if
        the maker had named a new day and called it good,

we are left so small, so shaken.

The Weightless Hum

Ode to the first few weeks

When *finally* you'd return
                    from an errand—another book
          of Auden, Derrida, or the small
                              canisters of oatmeal, dried apricots,
olives—your flat foot sounding down the corridor
was enough to flush my neck
                    with red pendants. You, too, felt it, would skirt
          table and chairs and land, at last,
                              on the divan, where we leaned
like great brown seals into each other's necks: sun-mottled,

brimming. What did we do

every day? Eat apricots, read
                    out loud, read for hours—
          your gentle throat throbbing,
                              earnest brow dark as a hem—and now,
after I have sunk full into your charity, is the time
to tell you: I forsook the poems, the essay's
                    bright mien, all that splendid brooding
          which truths be True: I confess,
                              dear heart, I was not listening
at all but practicing the weightless hum

of love, its incandescent

swim. Evenings, I studied sun
                    on the side of your face. I wanted,
          simple as a berry, to whisper,
                              Do you know, the way these slight
hairs shine, *right here*, you've the subtle halo of a question mark
for an ear? Just beyond our flat,
                    huge heads of blue hydrangea,
          summer-strewn, thronging the city
                              and someone playing Mendelssohn,
God love them, with every window thrown open.

Crying Over Onions

It's not the fumes. Not the purple tips like garish fingernails,
my bright knife shaving toward the board. It's you,
sitting, sagging like a struck tree on the new couch, the new
lampshade lit up, its methodical brown diagonals

thrown against the wall. My Cherokee great-aunt is full
of remedies, last week her mouth like an eyrie says *A-dohi* to you,
says, Fix him red onions, dear, in salad, stir-fry, sweet potato stew—
they're nature's truest antidepressant. But I'm a narwhal

tonight, long tooth spiraling before me, diving my 3000 feet
time and again, praying *Please, God*, praying *Do something,
you fucking onions, you caramelized pieces of shite*, make him

well. I call out like the town's bell tower for you to take your seat
and the plates steam, your chemicals eddy, a plumb line with string
enough to hold. *O Lord*, we bow, and I reach for you, I touch a single limb.

Why Every Man Should Knit

Of all the going-away presents, yours was by far
ne plus ultra. So it embarrasses you; what's not to praise?
It's good and true that a man should knit, your feyest
moil be wrapped around me now, so that, despite the war,

temerity, the epigone of leadership, market of fear,
the dying-in-the-arms-of, still births, blown limbs, our crazed
negligence which surely will erode us like the face
of that limestone statuette—goddess or kore—*Lady of Auxerre*,

I am, for a moment, happy. Brad, it's a happiness
borne of the unexpected *cum* generous, like looking
at Marianne Moore in that tri-corn hat she wore because,

she said, her head was lumpy. Is it right my husband gets
off the phone with you and weeps? This, too, a way of giving
thanks: an oblation for knowing you at all, an oblation for its cost.

III.

Take the emptiness you hold in your arms
and scatter it into the open spaces we breathe:
maybe the birds will feel how the air is thinner,
and fly with more affection.

—Rilke, from "The Duino Elegies"

Gallimaufry of Love

On the installation of a titanium mesh stint in my
father's heart

The body is ready; the body is down—below, like a lily's bulb.
Imagine the balloon they are making inside him: cutting-edge,
buttered with slow-release meds to dissolve the arterial blockage
that, one toothsome day, would kill him. Imagine how silent, how full

of blood my father is, brimming, the dark, mendicant fluid, culled
through that muscle we'd like to believe not in bondage
to the gallimaufry of love—but ardent nonetheless, a Caravagg-
ista who paints Holofernes' death spurting on Judith, powerful

temptress. You hero, heart! You hapless blood: exact bouillon of my father's
myocardium and Mariama Barrie's infibulated clitoris, blood from the skin
of labium minora and majora cut away. She, too, recumbent, the vulva's

aperture now sewn to the size of the tip of a matchstick, thin
as the hole that strained my father's vein to send its blood. Surgeries
make art of the body: marvel this canvas, age sixty-two; another, ten.

Finishing the House

My father swallowed a moon back in the 80s
                                    and did he ever shine
bulb-hot when he was mad and did he ever take his mind to a thing
   and turn it right-side-yes
                              with his hands: secondhand bikes
at Christmas, a nectar perch for Mother's birds, a Slip'N Slide
on the hill of our third acre, which was the only
                                             apology we got
   that time he challenged my kid brother to a fight and kicked me,
   gurgling a contrition he couldn't make out, away
                                        from his feet.
      Consider this word *irregardless*. I will put up the corner shelves
irregardless my father's
                        black hair painted into the terracotta wall,
      though today he's 14 hours away
                                 in Indiana, preparing for another
day at school, pulling the knot of his tie, unwrapping a lozenge,
   kissing my mother with a tickle in his throat,
                                        nothing on his mind.
The week he drove down he painted every room but one, he woke
   in the dark, made coffee, opened a new package of roller naps.
      Consider the subtle mechanism of sorrow:
                                    do. And now the wall
with my father's hair, which will not stop being there, satin latexed
   to my house, a small lever undoing
                              his hand from my throat,
      just that once, seven years ago. He is states away, enunciating
for the Japanese children
                        who cannot say his name, perfecting
a tease and a grimace, turning over a word he loves
   to use, its useless prefix, its coming press, *Irregardless*,
   he used to say,
                  the trouble with you is you. *Little one*,
      he calls me now, though I am grown, *Sweet one*.

After Your Father's Fallen from the Roof and Not Broken a Thing

He received the book you sent about Gettysburg and though he does not
tell you this you know he'll read most of it before bedtime and on the phone

he is grateful, he recalls the family trip to Antietam and how you,
nine years old, dropped your ice cream cone on someone's grave,

but it's your mother who tells you he's forgotten what to feed the hummingbirds
and all week long he's called your sister by your name though this

is not the worst of it: the doctor says it's like a bruise on the brain
and while the aphasia and disorientation will diminish, some things

may be lost forever. What's great, your father tells you, is that he can't
remember what's lost. *It's that old bliss they tell you about*, he says,

not knowing what you don't know you knew. After you hang up, you do not
cry like you thought you might, instead you get tangled in something

like prayer: what may be gone from him is last summer's drive to Tennessee,
hiking through white pine to the top of a mist-hung hill or perhaps

the paddy in Vietnam where a bullet struck his hip and flares smoked red
over the coming boats or perhaps the first time he touched your mother, or Hebrew,

or the color wheel, *Star Wars*, your brother's birth, the day he pulled
the mower over his foot, stuck in a gopher hole, toes-up. If last week God

held your father's body those twelve unconscious feet, you figure it's your job
to ask which things are shucked from his mind: your mouth, however,

has become a wide place, your tongue a useless oar, and looking down you see
your hands are the real supplicants, palms up, as if holding cantaloupe on your lap,

and when you fall asleep you dream a stretch of dandelions, some
whispering out thistle-tops in a pattern like rain, some smudging

across your skin that dewy, ocher language you cannot decipher.

Cylinder of Lies

First on the scene, you found her minutes from dead,
      a head of lettuce pressed to the dash and her purse spilled
like blood, *What are we doing here, Phineas,* she asked, *you and me,*

we got apples to pick. He must have been no older than you, thatch of hair
      gone dark with winter, the careful touch of a mulch spreader, that morning
it was you she knew without knowing you at all, musky with daybreak,

it was you held forth from the shawl of her end: the heart's soft ball
      unraveling as the car careened and struck the divide and when you
appeared, hallelujah-amen, tender cylinder of lies, she would not

let go your hand, whoever you were, her last, reassuring mistake. Given
      over now, as you are, to your fourth MRI, to the long tube that will
fail you once more, each of your doctors whitely mystified—it is not time

to think of her death but, instead, of Phineas: warm delusion,
      opening the darkest moment of that woman's life like a vault to send
a strobe of light thin and stubbled as the cornflower's stalk. What

questions wouldn't dribble to your lips? Someone says *Proceed,*
      your rutted song still as it can be so only the mind will mouth,
Well, Lord. No murmuring, Papi. Settle in, send your whole body

down, down into Franck's sonatas, cello rivering the brain. Listen
      close. At the end of track three, you can hear
Jacqueline du Pré's exhalation just below the bow, quiet as a stem.

Everybody Must Pass Stones

My father is thrilled with himself, drones the line
into the phone with Dylan's thronged rhythm, voice
thin and buoyant as his undershirts in the wash
or the cowl of my mother's hair, spun these sixty years
to a fine, airy thread, white as a peaked bulb
of light.   Nothing can disappoint him today, not
my single hiccup of laughter, not the stretch of pain below his navel
signaling another stone, another passing long
as his streak of shitty luck.   Where he sits in the dim family room,
his sciatica vibrated by a remote-controlled
lounge chair the size of Bimini, that soft huff and turn
of vowels means another set of pedants discuss canine acuity
on TV, that slender whip of fabric means he was called
to substitute today, knotted a tie and himself administered the last
of the state tests, holding one palm against the front loop
of his belt so as not to *let on*.   No one has to tell me
his high cheeks, more like Sitting Bull's than Custer's, are not ruddy.   Forty
years ago, the scapegrace of Pasadena, my father spoke
over the roar of the Pacific with pebbles in his mouth, roped
a surfboard to the Datsun he bought by picking oranges
every muggy summer of his youth, picked up girls
in broom skirts and bangles who'd hitch from San Francisco and take
a crack at variations of his weed: Bilbo, Frodo,
Meriwether, Sam.   How hobbled now, arthritic, smears
of blood in his urine, a cardiovascular bedlam, how
muscular only his sang-froid, granted these past thirty years
by the Synoptic Gospels.   My father, granite-faced when his fingers skimmed
names he knew, men from his platoon etched
into black stone polished shiny as a spoon, now tends to tear up
at each of the minor holidays when my mother
props a card on his pillow.   *My Nicked Miracle*, one begins,
My One and Lonely.   High today on pain's tart creed, he trombones,
he tambourines his borrowed song, cuts from the bridge
to urge, *All together now!* So we cough the line out
a final time, and where I mean to laugh, I'm able.

Dashed to Pieces like the Potter's Vessel

Your kidney is a dream-sac of old hurts: in stray electrolytes
they find your husband's early death, Lucille's, Pete's,
the acres of tobacco Thom stole from you and his third DUI,
not to mention the frost that took your cherry tree.

Soon you'll sleep, Coleridge will tell you
to which imagination the morning mist belongs,
from how many skies your surgeon borrowed blue,
when *ache* will ease to *itch*. The body is a potsherd's song:

it lets go its battered wives, its dilapidated preacher's
suits, praise be, but does anything in these terms soothe?
Here, Gran, it's raining hard, streets starting at the edges
to eddy. This morning we sit on the porch, kettle of a roof

harkening. Our neighbor boy walks by, wringing out
his shirt, shouts up to us, *Look at me, I'm soppy wet.*

It's Bright as Heaven out Here

For my Abuelo, Lamar

Ten minutes after I find out / you're in a coma
my best friend / in the entire state of Florida spots
a Black Widow spider and we / squat in the heat,
scared and awestruck, its red / hourglass belly-up,
suspended by eight legs / like crooked bobby pins,
and she says, *Well* / *we can't just leave it here.*
Oh yes we can, I think— / instead I say,
What should we do? / since she's the kind of woman
who will know and since I'm / baffled
that after your doctors / predicted by the angiogram
you'd be good for years, / a kidney infection
sent you straight on your way / to buying the farm.
My friend / heads across the street into a store where
some nitwit hands her / a bookmark to squash the spider
and she says, *Lady,* / *it's a Black Widow,*
which lands her one of those / question-marky smiles
and when she comes out / shaking her head we both know
it's no good, neither of us / covered by HMO or given to jolts
of bravery: we'll let the spider / be, right here
in the middle of everything, / snapdragons,
Border Collies, all these / oblivious people who might
stretch out an ankle / or set their toes on this gatepost
and locate, painfully, two tiny / pricks for which they'll cuss
and stamp / and find themselves, in an hour or two,
full of pus and hot blood. / It's bright as heaven out here
and we're starting to sweat, / weighing all this,
when my best friend / in the entire state of Florida takes
the apple from my hand / and brings it down, just like that,
on the Black Widow spider, / spurting it open. It was something to see,
Papa, our chests heaving, our / eyes stuck on that apple,
which I did not eat for lunch, / which we left right there
in the park, / wedged in the bars of the gate, covered
in broke-free pieces of web, / and I thought maybe
you'd like to know of it, / hovering as you are, between
here and there, how what / needs to happen will happen,
even if it surprises the breath / right out of you.

In the Middle of a Long Illness

Sex, especially, seems stupid, the elaborate writhing, bodies spurting
within and without: this, when nauseated, is not even funny, is bright,

slick, burnt as the green acid you spit up an hour ago, which at least
you can joke about—not *having the guts* to vomit with sincerity these days,

eating so little you almost don't remember how lovely the avocado is,
diced with boiled egg, set delicately atop a slice of cheese, on bread,

with salt. Sometimes, it's true, you dream of food, though instead of smelling
or tasting fruits, pastries, legumes, you have emotional encounters

with them, they resemble family members, are sweet to you on the phone,
chide with livid tones the long, low ache in the center of your kidney.

Mostly, you want to read. Mostly, you can't: thanks to vertiginous meds
the sentences squirm like teenagers in church. To this end, you've

taken to watching birds, can now distinguish Nuthatch from Swallow,
Merganser from Scoter, but this you don't discuss with anyone

but your father, who could tell you color, call, diet, and mating season
of every last bird in the northern hemisphere. When you're sick,

nobody stops you from exaggeration. On good days your husband
takes you for a drive, though not in the manual, which makes you queasy,

and only when you can roll the window down, stick a bare foot out.
Yesterday you saw a priest at the wheel of a Chevrolet the color

of a band-aid, a woman dangerously pregnant carrying a sack
of grapefruit, and, at the Broken Spoke, someone with a shovel chasing

someone with a stick. Besides suppositories, what you hate most is
beer commercials. Everybody's so damn radiant. You never say this aloud,

though you could, being granted, at present, inordinate rites to bellyache—
you know it's a trick, you know it's not radiance you hate, nor the snow-crusted

shoulders of the girls who never stop laughing or the boys at their sides
having, inevitably, said the right thing: it's you, whole glitches of your heart

holding forth, how you've begun to stop yourself from laughing. This evening
when your husband rinses your hair with a grace you call *nightingale*,

he will have a sneezing fit, his body barking round after round of flecked air,
his face a consortium of news, and you will want to snigger, you will want

to splash him, join him in the only bacchanalia left in your lives. Instead
you will say, *A su salud, salud,* as many times as it takes, reaching

as an indifferent wing for your towel. But during the particularly endless
midnight when the people of beer commercials make their handsome march

across your mind, your crow-eyed jealousy will make you smirk; the smirk
will leak into the dark like an unstoppered perfume. *You fool—*

you don't even like to ski. This is when you'll tilt your head
toward your husband and make out his mouth by the window's light,

how the petals of his breath open and close. How he blooms without trying.

On Marrying Someone Better Looking than Me, Which isn't a Feat, Really, but Worth Noting

He does not suffer well. This is because he is beautiful, astounding
        as the eye of a peacock feather
     tinctured blue and green, feathers within feathers,
    shivering, a beauty beyond what even he is aware,
cheekbones sheltering the glory of his ductless spleen, the blood's
        able proteins, each cell's flagellar motor,
      yes, down to that detail,
    and yes, too, with that in mind, every buckle of the spine chicaning
its Grecian looks up the neck to the brow, the nose, lashes
        giraffe-long over the open tide, what could be
     sea-gray or sea-green of his eyes
    and what's more is *his own unknowing*, though in some yawning
pocket of that sundown body—perhaps his finger's crease—
        he must be aware of it, a magnificence most of us
    can only fathom: umber,
   buttery ribbon of firefly's gut, weathervane's volte-face,
the rent of virility over the orchard from last year's fire, and now,
        his whole head hot as paraffin wax, ears
     red-tipped mangoes ripening
   on the sill, lips a pallid *clair de lune*, he offers music, he's brimming
with it: accordion lungs, carotid viola, toms of phlegm like lungs
        themselves, bless him, my stunning husband
    prostrate beside me, tacit, grumpy
   as peat bog, willing the bronchial tubes to muscilate, to sleep
so hard the bonnyclabber will not bother—this man
        whose even bilious corners speak enzyme, rhizome—
    will wake tomorrow feeling
   not a lick better, will rasp among the antibodies, silt my hand
to his cheek and say to my fingers as if fiber-optic points of distress,
       Principessa, have you any broth of bone
    for me? And when I bring a tray, steaming
   with soup, a single Cymbidium orchid tucked beneath
his spoon, he'll sit up slowly, gazing into the bowl
        with a forlorn welcome for his own face, and speak
    some ancient prayer aloud:
To the One, he says, Before Whom All Words Recoil.

Man as Walnut

Head thrown back, he cries, is not ashamed,
though his people are farmers and lawyers. He hollows
out the nadir for sounds: the spine's delicate
nuggets, the tiny pear of green gall, a miserable wonder
locked in his body and sent to the throat, that petty thief
of the spirit hawking its calamities. He works
at making what noises he must, stays at it, drooping
like the sunflower heavy with kernels. Here
with the sheets pulled taut I have thought to gather
what falls, antediluvian as a psalm, but all that will emerge
true as the translucent paper halving a small meat
is this: were each of us to know this weeping
and let ourselves, what would not come
undone, whole, unhulled, from the sky?

IV.

*And the miraculous comes so close
to the ruined, dirty houses—
something not known to anyone at all,
but wild in our breast for centuries.*

—Anna Akhmatova, "Everything is Plundered"

You Look across the Earth and See

To my tallest lover, who also thinks W.B. Yeats kicks ass

Tell me you've found the wind to help hear all things loud and beautiful,
a line that jangles from the mouth that lifts it up, or falling from the pigeons,

each and every one who sings *When you are old and gray and full of sleep*—
tell me you note the fragile, yes, the wretched and unyielding things: small

and stiff, a lady's legs held tight together at her bony knees and kept
together ankle-tight. Tell me up there is not an everywhere *the ceremony*

of innocence is drowned or is it that you look across the earth and see the four
who've hatched and grown from Leda's eggs? Are you the closer to Byzantium

than we who walk down here with air as dull as breath, as sweet and stale
as those who now have just deserted it? Tell me to seek Athena's eyes

of gray, tell me to aim for *femme fatale*, to loom as big as you, if only in their minds,
the dead. What happens to the girls born of the swan? But for those gentle

hands, who would you be? You, man who found your body long one day,
the way I found my body small and knew that I should notice

all things tall and wild, tell me Unleash The Brigand God, held cold
and endless as the sky, as cold and restless as ourselves, all we who seek

the bee-loud glade: it does us good—doesn't it?—to sleep, to old, to gray.

When Love First Brought Its Bumper Crop

I. Beloved of the Ground

      Start with your brother, not one to weep, at Eucharist, which itself began
as a Dark-eyed Junco into flight, ignorant of its own beauty

            but flickering up and plunging with a surety that frightens
      you and your solid body, stuck all these years in shoes and a bloody
nose. All of us, our quarried years, Beloved of the Ground. He didn't

            mean to, your brother tells you, though he knew it was coming, that dark,
sweet pressure snaking its way from knuckles and beltways of the body

            to a pure burst beneath muscles of the face, the kind of cry
      you both know *el corazón* alone cannot create. When they ask, you should not
begin with the beginning. It is unwise but most of all untrue,

            for who is to say when love first brought its bumper crop:
dried rows of corn shushing an August storm, the stream you

            trespassed Fergie Ladd's land to get to, its tadpoles billioning
      in the heat, your drawing pad soggy at the edges and your sister offering
the last of the boysenberries from the deep red bottom

            of her pocket. Why shouldn't it have begun here, starlings en masse
over the soybeans and not even the scarecrow willing them, *Go.* Which rustle
            opened the speckled egg of your heart?

II. Half a Wing Yet

      The first and only laugh you got from the Welch boy, his blond hair
and blond arms: the best part of Sunday meetings, you with your body

           half a wing yet, your mouth a gaudy nest, wits, insinuations. No,
      your mouth a pardoned bulb, the harvest moon, held in place
by the seasons and the wrong sun turning you slowly, slowly to a woman.

III. On the Occasion of a Good-bye

Where this one is going, away from the drastic angles of your new love,
a natural grief settles, spiraling below the jack-o'-lanterns and potted

azalea on the porch, that bricked sheet announcing where *home*
begins. At the airport when he leaned against the wall in beleaguered good-bye,
you could see certain verticals shake loose: he unfolds from the pencil-upright

world for the moment you'll come together again, a moment held forth,
split apart not like a flag but nimbus—an anticipation one might call foresight

or fancy. Here in Oklahoma, at your gate, D14, something has happened;
what you'd identify as the horizon has bumbled its perpendiculars, its diagonals,
so after all it's not the horizon but a terrific set of elisions: someone's

elbow resting on a table, someone's chin fitted to a palm. Between
table and chin: strata, so many planes, so many hands, connected by all

we've left out, like the ball joint of bone, the stalk of forearm. You see
yourself as a matter of standing tiers, each with its long rod of geometries—
intricate beginnings and endings marked perhaps by point A or point B,

by horizontals, the meaty betrayal of surface after surface. Even now
the gathering cumuli understand themselves, their heavy spread,

their dark stomachs, which makes you brave, which is surprising.
The sky rumbles around the leaving sun and if you both stand still enough,
not touching any other thing, your bodies thinly pointing—him stopped

on his way to wherever he parked; you in a windowed dome, conduits,
fallen light, people all around who have known for years what you, too,

will find: the heavens are not a covering holding in the earth's
hair but another example of collision—one surface settling, one rising,
each plane an explosive set of points meant to send you their brief explanation:

moon, morning, cloud.

IV. Thin Legs of Birds

Here, too, a particular beginning: you kept a plum in your hand
the whole day, pressed it to your mouth, not to eat but to smell—to smell!

Somber corm, Lenten round, good as a flower
to your face: anything worthwhile in this world has taken a patience
you didn't know you had, a dare, Western wind in your hair, all the days of June

between your thighs. You and the red-faced
cormorant at the playground where you pitched a swing in the air

and, for last night, prayed forgiveness. When it came,
you and the plum rejoiced. The plum itself was forgiveness,
a gift: mouthful, rivulets, palm back, pit. He, too, a gift,

this one you'd marry, and its beginning, like the priest
intoning, elements in hand, lifted slow, precative: tree, field, bird,

those bowls and bowls of beans to snap. No wonder
you don't remember who was there, each opus of grin and wink, while
clambering back to you now, the words of the first hymn you rose from your knees

to sing—its doe-eyed rhymes reaching all, all the way
to the stained glass, and how, perhaps, if you didn't know

any better, you'd guess with those careful particles of light
the dusk is itself "Thou Fount of Every Blessing," come for you,
come for him, richer than you'll ever be again, plumb daft

with joy, your vows sprung from the pulp
of clouds, dense as stem and sprout, radish-deep in the humus

of love. There, in that silly white dress, a pouf of Ptolemy's
eighth heaven, you, too, cried and knelt and offered your promises
and prayers. You felt the thin legs of birds atop your ankles.

V. The Sound of Seeds

All those risking wings, their fey, able ways, aren't they at least
a little like ours? No, not us, feet as good as gills,

whole cavities of ourselves turkey-waddled,
unable to lark from the mount, the skiff, from stage or sidewalk,
to God, from God, or maybe just the sun, for now: O Watchful

Sky, O Lifted Head—guineafowl, buttonquail, oriele,
thrush. Crossbil, siskin, greenfinch, goldfinch, rubythroat,

rubythroat, wren. Long before you woke to the spore-thick
air, before you spotted yourself wandering about
in the fireflied night—even before you listened for the sound of seeds

blushing open to soil, you in your silent places began to shed
the fist-sized sac each month, *la regla*, like molting your blood came down.

This was one beginning; your mother gave a happy
yelp, your father whispered, *Salud, salud*. Do not catalogue your fallings
apart: God, sky, grains, loves, each start one part ending. This time,

hands taut across their chests like small fans, pink and copper,
they ask, *when*, when did it begin? You, smaller, pinker, copper, must know,

but not for the knowing, must say, but not for the saying.

Sweetly from the Tree

Listen, stamen: your surrender is just a beginning,
the spinous distance between desire and the quiet
clinch of satisfaction. Take the hexagon, how it
will fill, fanned with wings that mean to bring

April's nascent truths. In winter, I will not ask
where the bees have gone. I will walk to the grove
in my old boots and give ear. Littlest of lovers,
vested in pistil and comb, I speak now to you: dance

your tremble. Perhaps you of all, not drone but roamer, know
what purple means—given, some morning darker than

the human hymn of misgivings, you turn home
and make there what the orchid could not, alone.

Only your precision is a secret: prism of nectar, haven of gold—
I want what you want, and the stamen, and the sun.

Acknowledgments:

Grateful acknowledgment is made to the following journals in which some of the works in this book first appeared, sometimes in slightly different versions or under different titles:

Alaska Quarterly Review: "Serpentine"

Avatar Review: "Halfway to the Jesse James Wax Museum," "Everybody Must Pass Stones"

Bellingham Review: "The Lanterns"

Books & Culture: "Dashed to Pieces like the Potter's Vessel," "Sweetly from the Tree"

Christianity & Literature: "Man as Walnut," "In the Pocket of Your Winter Coat"

Cimarron Review: "Instructions for the Twitterpated, Nightingaled, and Sore in Love"

Colorado Review: "The Hyssop Tub"

Dogwood: "In the Middle of a Long Illness," "The Wry World Shakes Its Head"

Fugue: "The Green Spider," "Love, Anonymous," "All Hallow Even"

GSU Review: "Torn"

Goodfoot: "Just like Solomon"

The Grove Review: "The Necessary Dark"

Hayden's Ferry Review: "Cylinder of Lies"

IMAGE: "After Your Father's Fallen from the Roof and Not Broken a Thing"

Indiana Review: "Mother as Opalescent Bottle"

MARGIE: "What's Done"

Mars Hill Review: "Of Course I Hit at the Moon"

Missouri Review: "Finishing the House"

Perspectives: "A Note to Martin Luther King, Jr. Regarding the Use of Certain Transitive and Intransitive Verbs"

Rock & Sling: "It's Bright as Heaven out Here"

Ruminate: "On Marrying Someone Better Looking than Me, Which isn't a Feat, Really, but Worth Noting," "The Weightless Hum"

The Southern Review: "When Love First Brought Its Bumper Crop"

Stonework: "Mother as Water-Damaged Book"

Tampa Review: "Weaving," "Architecture of an Apology"

Valparaiso Poetry Review: "Why Every Man Should Knit"

"Fetching" was first published in *And Know This Place: Poetry of Indiana* by Indiana Historical Society Press.

"Sweetly from the Tree" was first printed as a part of a limited edition print series by DM Stith in collaboration with Indiana University.

The author wishes to thank Barbara Hamby, whose care and attention to my work has shaped and propelled it and whose kindness has made me a better writer and a better person; David Kirby, James Kimbrell, Barbara Hamby, Nancy Warren, and Amy Koehlinger for reading the earliest version of this manuscript and still allowing me to graduate; Jennifer Perrine, Sara Pennington, Tom Hunley, Walt Wangerin, Allison Schuette, Michael Mobley, Wendy Shreffler, Jennifer Maier, and Steve Gherke for working with me on parts or the whole of this book; Heather Sellers and Mary Brown for good counsel and courage; Florida State University for the Kingsbury Fellowship and the Lilly Fellows Program for a post-doctoral fellowship, both of which allowed me to complete this book and pursue its publication; to the good folks at New Issues, especially Bill and Marianne, for giving it a go; and to Joshua: for believing.

Photo by Chris Cox

Susanna Childress holds a Master's from the University of
Texas at Austin and a PhD from Florida State University.
Her first book, *Jagged with Love*, was awarded the
Brittingham Prize in Poetry from the University of Wisconsin
and the Devil's Kitchen Reading Award from the University
of Southern Illinois-Carbondale. She has received an AWP
Intro Journals Award, the National Career Award in Poetry
from the National Society of Arts and Letters, and a Lilly
post-doctoral fellowship. She lives in Holland, Michigan.